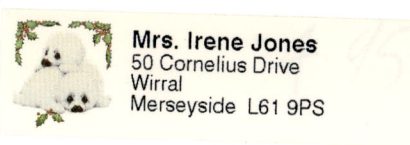

Mrs. Irene Jones
50 Cornelius Drive
Wirral
Merseyside L61 9PS

CW01549824

POEMS OF A
BIBLICAL NATURE

POEMS OF A BIBLICAL NATURE

Arthur McKenzie

VANTAGE PRESS
New York

FIRST EDITION

All rights reserved, including the right of
reproduction in whole or in part in any form.

Copyright © 1995 by Arthur McKenzie

Published by Vantage Press, Inc.
516 West 34th Street, New York, New York 10001

Manufactured in the United States of America
ISBN: 0-533-11136-6

Library of Congress Catalog Card No.: 94-90213

0 9 8 7 6 5 4 3 2 1

To my son Robin and his family,
who are
engaged in the Lord's service
on the mission field

Contents

Noah and the Flood	1
Jacob and Esau	5
Joseph and His Brothers	9
Joseph Made a Slave	14
Joseph in Prison	19
Joseph Rises to Fame	23
Joseph Reunited with His Family	26
Pharaoh and the Plagues of Egypt	33
Gideon	44
David the Shepherd	49
Esther	53
Shadrach, Meshach, and Abed-nego	63
The Writing on the Wall	69
Jonah	72
Choice	77
Don't Miss the Bus	78
Join the Queue	80
The Piper	81

POEMS OF A
BIBLICAL NATURE

Noah and the Flood

Day by day Noah hammered away, as plank by plank he laid,
While people mocked, others scoffed, and some just stayed and played.
But Noah he preached that judgement would fall on this wicked race;
But man he has a free will, setting his own direction and pace.

They laughed at Noah as he pegged the planks, saying, "Oh no, no thanks,
You've told us all this before; and you, Noah, you think you know the score!"
But Noah, he trusted God and laboured day by day, and still he gave his message
Whatever the crowds might say.

"This land is watered by the dew; and that's without a doubt,
So what's this rain and water you keep telling us all about?
It sounds crazy, crazy as your boat and its crew."
Noah would shake his old head, and heave a sigh of despair.

"If you people would only realise your danger and listen to what I share.
There is a way out as I repeatedly shout, believe, and turn from your evil ways.
For our God, He has the answer: He cares, and He loves, and He saves.
This boat that He would have me build is a means of our salvation.
It's God's provision and a means—a means to save our nation."

Noah, he gathered the animals, gathered them from far and near,
One stubborn old ass, he kicked and pranced, and the crowd let
 up a cheer.
But that stubborn old ass was chosen. It was the crowd that
 needed to fear.

"Still at it, Noah?" shouted one man, just so the others would
 laugh.
He was the joker in the crowd, and to the applause took off his
 hat.
Then for an encore he shouted, "No rain today, I see;
It's only wet in the river, and a great deal more in the sea."

The Ark was nearing completion, for Methuselah was getting old;
Noah loaded the Ark, as instructed, for he did just what he was
 told.
At last the Ark was laden, with food, water, grain, and hay,
Then the animals, two by two; old Noah, he led the way.

"Come on, wife, and family. Ham, Japhet, Shem, bring your bits,
And belongings—oh, and your wives, don't forget them!"
Once in the Ark they settled, and God, He closed the door;
And what God shuts, no man opens—if he tries for evermore.

The spectators were there as usual, waiting to have their fun,
But for them the show was over, for Noah it had just begun.
"What's that I felt?" said the joker. "As if someone spat in my
 eye.
It's not a tear I know, for I very seldom cry."

"I felt it too!" said a woman. "It fell right from the sky."
Then a fear came on them; what if Noah was right?
What if God was judging? It gave them quite a fright.
"It can't be," said an egotist. "I felt it once before when I was
By a waterfall and, of course, I know the score!"

But the fountains of the deeps were opened, and darkness filled
    the skies.
Down came the rain in torrents, as the waters began to rise.
The crowd was in a panic, running to and fro, trying to find a dry
    spot,
But there was nowhere they could go.

"Noah, you were right! Please help us!" as they hammered on
    the door.
"Open up, open up, dear Noah, we'll ridicule you no more."
But the day of grace was over, and God had shut the door.

The Ark it gently lifted, as the waters they rose higher;
People climbed up the mountains, but the flood rose even higher.
The people, they were drowned: fathers, sons, mothers, and
    daughters.
Each one to an eternity, beneath the rising waters.

All people perished beneath the waves except Noah and his
    family,
They were saved because they trusted in God's promises, and
    followed His direction.
We men are not perfect, but He will bring us to His perfection.

This story is an old one, antediluvian we may say, because it's
    about
Things before the Flood, but the message is still for today.
We don't even have to look around us, to see the wickedness,
On every side, surround us, we have been warned repeatedly.

But do we heed that warning? We are rapidly approaching
The midnight hour, and where will you be in the morning?
As Noah's Ark was his salvation, we have Jesus to save our nation.
And Jesus died for all mankind, not just a few.
He has saved me. Now how about you?

Jacob and Esau

Now Rebekah was expecting (that's Isaac's wife, you know).
And he himself was happy, as he wandered to and fro;
For God had promised his father (Abraham), to make him father of many nations,
And Isaac was the son of the promise, hence the great elations.

Rebekah went into her tent, for her time was drawing near;
Her serving woman in attendance, what had she to fear?
For it's faith in God that triumphs, it's faith in God, that wins,
And God increased her blessings, for God He gave her twins.

Esau was her first-born, and amid her joy, and squeals,
As Jacob followed soon after, directly on Esau's heels.
Isaac was delighted, as he held his first-born lad.
"Great work, lass," he chanted, "you've made me a double dad."

Esau was Isaac's favourite, and Jacob his mother's boy.
In a family, there should be no favourites, for a child is not a toy!
The boys grew up, as boys do, each had his separate choice,
Esau wandered as a hunter, and Jacob a shepherd, within the sound of his mother's voice.

One day returning from the hunt, being very weary . . . Esau flopped right on the ground.
His brother, Jacob, was busily stirring, an appetising pottage of lentils, that he'd found.
"Give me to eat, my brother, lest from fatigue, I die."
Jacob carefully rubbed his hands, and looked him in the eye.

"I'll trade you my bread and pottage, which will restore your
    ebbed-out might,
For your birthright, my brother dear."
Esau groaned aloud, but gave in, without a fight!

The years went by, and Isaac aged, the sight of his eyes grew
    dimmer,
But his taste buds, they were blossoming, not making him any
    thinner.
He smacked his gums, as he called his boy, "Esau, please come
    quick.
Make your old dad some venison stew, make it good, and make
    it thick.

"Off you go a-hunting, and catch a fine young deer;
Then I'll give you my blessing, lad; of that, just have no fear."
But Rebekah was within earshot, as sometimes a wife may be.
You don't need a keyhole for listening, in a tent; you just look,
    and see.

Rebekah slipped out to the paddock, for she knew where Jacob
    would be.
"Quick, lad, kill two young kids, and I'll tell you just what I'll do,
I'll chop up herbs and veges, and make you my finest stew.
For your father's just promised his blessing to Esau, if he'll make
Him his favourite broth. But I'll make you, my famous stew,
One smell of it, will make his taste buds froth;
And bring me their skins, and I'll fashion for you;
I'll fashion you, a hirsute suit, for your brother
Is rough and hairy, and his smell is that of a brute."

Now Jacob (whose name means supplanter), readily agreed to the plan,
And although you cannot deceive God, you can sometimes deceive a man.
His nearly blind father, was suspicious; when Jacob's voice he heard,
Greeting Isaac in a dutiful manner, saying, "This is your broth, Dad, I've just prepared."

Old Isaac bade him come closer, so he could establish the fact,
Which of his sons carried the basin, and in accordance would know how to act.
Running his hands over his son's neck, which was really a goat-skin vest,
He said, "Your voice is that of Jacob, but your hair and smell pass the test."

So Jacob received the blessing, he had supplanted his brother's right,
By deception, and his mother's connivance, he reckoned, he'd be in for a fight.

Just then Esau returned from his trip—and put on the cauldron to boil.
He then prepared his venison, cutting it very small.
His father liked the meaty taste, but found it hard to chew,
So like a good son, he laboured, without too much ado.

All his efforts he found were useless, for his brother had beaten him to it.
He banged with his fists on the table, saying, "Some day our Jacob will rue it."
Meanwhile Rebekah all agitated, hastened to find her son.
"Oh, Jacob dear, please pack your bags, for I fear you'll have to run.

"Go to my brother Laban, he lives quite a distance away,
Here's some drink and some sandwiches—get going, and don't delay,
For your brother has threatened to kill you;
When your father has passed away."

Now Jacob needed no second bidding, to put distance between himself and his tent.
For he knew his brother's temper, and he knew Esau,
And he knew that he would not relent.
And what happened next is a long long story!

But what have we learned so far, from this teaching?
Christians, you've been born again, so don't sell your birthright,
For a pottage of this messy world.
You've accepted Christ's banner. So let it be unfurled.
And, parents, no favourites please, for God has no favourites,
His sun shines on the just, and unrighteous alike.

Incidentally, Jacob became Israel and Esau the Amalekite.

Joseph and His Brothers

Joseph was a happy lad, he had his brothers, and he had his dad,
Mother and sister too, I might add, but something happened, and that was bad!
When he was born, his father was getting on; and as Rachel was his dad's
Favourite wife, he, Joseph, became his, Jacob's, favourite son.
Favouritism again, had raised its head, as it has happened many times before,
And favouritism can cause envy, strife, and hatred, whether you're rich
Or whether you're poor.

The elder brothers were working men, and went to tend their sheep,
Whilst he being young, just stayed at home, and played at hide-and-seek.
One day Jacob said to him, "Joseph my fine lad, I've a surprise for you.
It's hidden in the hay, so off you go and seek it; it's some clothing—
Now nothing else I'll say."

Joseph ran off all jubilant, for he was a happy boy,
For his dad was so good to him, and he was full of joy.
Joseph could hardly believe his eyes, when a new coat he found,
There it lay beneath the hay, lying upon the ground.
"Oh, Dad, you're so good to me, I love you such a lot,
What a surprise you have for me, and look at the colours that it's got.
They're so fine, they're dazzling, I'm so happy I could sing.
Off I'll go and show my coat, to my brothers, but honest, Dad, I'll not gloat."

The brothers could hardly their feelings hide, at Joseph's radiant face,
Which they themselves mistook for pride.
"You're a favourite, you're a schemer, you'll tell us next that you're a dreamer."
"Yes, I am," Joseph said, "I dreamt the other night that I was with you in the fields
Collecting the sheaves of corn, and mine stood up, while yours fell down
And bowed to mine, and they were looking all forlorn."

The brothers, they stood speechless, trying to conceal their rage.
What their younger brother suggested, and with such audacity—that they would bow
To him! He needed locking up; he needed to be placed in a cage.
Their time would come, and he would see, just what they thought of him.

Sometime later, Joseph had another dream, which he felt that he must tell.
"We were all stars in the sky, but my star did the brightest shine,
While yours were all duller, and bowed to mine, even the sun and moon
They took their turn, to pay their homage, to my brilliant shine."

"Enough of this talk," his father said. "If you think that your parents,
And brethren are going to bow down to you, think again, lad,
For it's not true. You're only a young one, and remember that,
It was bad enough with your sheaves of corn,
But this heavenly vision I must scorn; as we're your parents, you are
Subjected to us, so off to bed and without any fuss."

"Sorry, Dad, but if you only knew, it's the second dream, so it
   must be true!"

As Jospeh grew older, he'd more chores to do, his playing days
   were over.
He was still a favourite—that is true, but no longer lived in
   clover.
One day his father said to him, "Put on your colorful coat, and off
And take these victuals to your brothers. They are away with the
   sheep
At Shechem, or some other place remote."
"Righto, Dad, see you later," Joseph said as he picked up the
   load.
"God's blessings, son," his father said, not knowing what
   forbode.

"Someone's approaching," Reuben said. "I wonder just who it
   can be?"
(Then Joseph appeared on the horizon.) "No! Oh no! But I think
   it must be he."
"It's our brother," said Simeon to Judah, "and that I can plainly
   see."
All the others looked in Joseph's direction. "And what does he
   want with us now?
To tell us his latest dream, or come boasting, or show off that
   coat somehow!"

"What shall we do with him, now it's our turn?" said one of the
   brothers quickly.
"Let's kill that dreamer," someone chanted. Poor Reuben gulped,
Rose up and left, for he was feeling sickly.
"He's brought us food, so let's eat first; he has his uses, you see.
Here's a pit—let's put him in it—and talk while we drink our tea,
But let's remove his coat first, for it cost a pretty penny."

Judah spoke up by saying . . . "No, you don't—don't you . . . kill him, for he's
Part of our family, after all—he is our brother—and without him,
We'd have some explaining to do. I think we, can make a profit
If we consider it carefully.
There's a caravan of Ishmaelite traders rapidly approaching this spot.
Let's offer to sell them our brother—just wait till they see what we've got."

"*Salamat alicum*," they greeted. "We've got something to trade—
A fine strapping youth, and a strong one,
Wait till you see how he's made."
The haggling was soon over, with all parties content with their deal—
The brothers twenty coins richer—and the Ishmaelites shook hands on the deal.
They all forgot poor Joseph. Now how do you think he'd feel?

The brothers took a kid and killed it, and in the blood, dipped Joseph's coat—
Then hastily packed up, and moved to another spot, quite remote.
Reuben came back to their old campsite and went straight away to the pit.
"Joseph," he called. "It's Reuben—please grab hold of this stick."
He called again—but no answer, then he became quite sick;
For looking around, there on the ground, was a dried pool of blood, very thick.

He staggered to his feet, and trudged on, till he met the rest of his kin.
"Why, oh why, did you . . . you've killed him, you know it is very bad.
And as you know, I'm the eldest, and will have to answer to Dad."
"Hold your horses, don't panic so, Reuben; listen and hold out your hand.
We did not kill Joseph our brother, but sold him to an Ishmaelite band.
We made a profit, now here's your share, it's not as if we didn't care.
We just couldn't stand his dreams, for at times they clashed with our schemes."
"But what are we going to tell our dad, when we return, about his favourite lad?"
"Don't grieve so, don't take offence, we have his blood-stained coat, as evidence.
That some wild beast must have met the lad,
Your favourite son, we're so very sorry, Dad!"

So they returned with stricken faces, as a disguise—
Then they all shuffled in, and told their terrible lies.
Jacob was overcome with grief, when he heard their tale of woe,
"Oh, Joseph my son, no, no, no, I'll go down stricken
To the grave—Joseph my son, that nobody else could save."

The whole family went into mourning, the brothers too, without exception,
And so they continued their lying deception.
This story's not finished as you may know.
But it's all for now, as I have to go.

Joseph Made a Slave

A rope was tied to Joseph's wrist, which was attached to a camel's halter;
A grinning trader gave it a twist, saying, "Step out, lad, don't you falter."
Mile after weary mile he trudged, and the camel's pace was slow,
But that didn't seem to help him, for there were many more miles to go.

At night they stopped and made camp, preparing food and drink,
But Joseph didn't eat much, all he could do was think.
Why did the brothers hate him so? He was part of their kith and kin,
What wrong had he done them? He examined his every thought.
Perhaps he'd slipped up somewhere, in the things that he'd been taught,
Had he caused them to envy? Had he made them jealous of him?
He knew he was his father's favourite, because of favours shown to him.
Was it the dreams? Was it the multicoloured coat?
Was it because he didn't work? He didn't really mean to gloat.

"Father in heaven, I turn to you. You are the God of my father,
He taught me many things, and told me about his vision,
And the promise, that you gave him. I'll follow You, that is my decision.
I ask You to bless my brethren, and all those who are at home.
I ask You to bless my captors, with them I have to roam."
Then Joseph felt a great release, then he, Joseph, fell sound asleep.

Before it was light, he was awake, for there was movement in the camp.
The traders rose early, for they wished to move e'er it grew warm,
So they were packed, and on their way, just at the rise of dawn.
Joseph noticed less hostility, for they had talked the previous night—
It seemed that they all had something in common
For Abraham, was a forefather to the Jew and Ishmaelite.
From that day on, Joseph was permitted, to upon a camel ride,
To which was fitted a kind of seat, where he could be tied.
"You might try to escape," his captor said, as he tied the knots securely,
"You're worth a few shekels to me, you know, but if you escaped, well!
That would be a different story."

After a while, Joseph tried to smile, and said, "If I promise not to run,
Will you untie my wrists for me, for the rubbing of the rope's, not much fun.
And besides, when you sell me, how much profit will I bring?
If my wrists are cut through, I won't be worth a thing."
"Smart young man," the trader said. "It must run in your race,
For I've heard a tale of Jacob your father, who outsmarted his uncle Laban—
And he did it face to face."
So Joseph's wrists were untied, and said the trader with a grin,
"If I don't get my price for you in Egypt, I'll teach you my trade and win!"

The slave auction was going in full swing, and the wealthy had
    gathered around.
As the chief of Pharaoh's guard was present, the police were
    controlling the crowd.
One or two sales had been snips, going at bargain prices.
Then came the lot they'd been waiting for . . . it was the slave
From Canaan, the land of fruit and spices.

They started off at a good price, with many making a bid;
And then the bidding grew really hard—and Joseph was knocked
    down
To the captain of Pharaoh's guard.
While on the edge of the crowd, stood the traders, grinning so
    happily,
They rubbed their hands praising their gods, for they'd made a
    good profit, you see.

Joseph was escorted by a servant to the impressive home of
    Potiphar,
Saying that his master was a just man—that is, if you did your
    work.
But that he would show no mercy if your set task, you decided to
    shirk.
But Joseph had resolved from the very start that he would do his
    best,
"For whatsoever thy hand findeth to do, do it with all thy might."
And following that line with any task was bound to turn out right.

Joseph found that his master was just—and for his diligence, and
    trust,
He was rewarded. He was promoted to the key man—
The man in charge of the keys—his master trusted him,
For Joseph, trusted in God, and God blessed him,
And so his master's household prospered.

Now Potiphar's wife was fair to look upon, but she looked upon
    Joseph with great desire.
For he was a comely youth, whom she had to admire.
For she, being an Egyptian, thought as the Egyptians think.
In her cunning she would make him win her,
For she had set her heart on having an affair.

"Joseph, your master thinks very highly of you, so I, do too;
And there is a task you can perform for me, you can keep me
    company,
For when I'm all alone, I get very lonely.
And if you're good to me, I'll be good for you,
That's a good arrangement for both us two."

"Mistress, you are my master's wife, and I respect him greatly.
He's made me head over all his house, and I'll not cause him
    strife,
He's made me head over all his house, saving you, his wife."
"You'll be sorry, Joseph, of this I'll have you warned.
You don't know Egyptian women—especially if they've been
    scorned."

From then on Joseph kept his distance, but opportunities come to
    those
Who pursue them. Potiphar's wife just waited her chance
And saw her opportunity to lead Joseph in a merry dance.
Potiphar her husband was away on duty, so she discharged her
    servants.
"So now for you, Joseph—my Hebrew beauty.

"Joseph, we are all alone, my husband's away, and the servants have gone.
Come into my chamber, and with me stay, and I'll forget the other day."
"No, madam, t'would be a terrible sin against God, as well as betraying my master."
And with that he hurried past her, but not before
She grabbed his coat. "I'll get you. I'll make you pay. When Potiphar returns
I'll know what to say—insult me; would you?
You Hebrew slave—you could be my champion—but you're a knave."

When Potiphar returned, his wife told him her tale; she showed Joseph's coat
As evidence—then began to wail—Potiphar listened,
Saying, "Her tale it must be true, the evidence alone is incriminating,
And her added tears, they're corroborating."
When Joseph put up his defence, he was not believed, through evidence.
Potiphar passed his judgement, saying, "You have abused the position of trust, I placed
You in, so it's into the king's dungeon, because of your sin."
Poor Joseph found the judgement hard—and of slander—by which he'd been marred.
Clothing was his stumbling block. He'd suffered before, by wearing a coat,
And now having one snatched from him, it seemed as if whatever happened,
He wasn't going to win—but God was with Joseph,
And that's all that mattered to him.

Joseph in Prison

The prison was a large one, with many prisoners within.
For Pharaoh's word was law, and not to fulfil it, that indeed was sin.
Amongst the many inmates Joseph nodded to, or spoke a kindly word,
He found Pharaoh's baker and butler, who confided what had occurred.
They were in for some misdemeanour, or so they said they were.
So they had just resigned themselves to their present state of affairs.

Joseph as he languished within the prison cell . . . thought
Of all the things that had happened . . . oh, the tales, that he could tell.
But he had no one to talk to, except the other men,
And they had woes of their own, but they'd listen now and then.

But Joseph had great faith, in his Father God, in heaven.
He prayed to Him continually, both in and out of season.
He didn't know why he was in there, but he knew that God had His reason.
His faith grew stronger, but it was often tested.
Some would listen, others laughed, while others grinned and jested.
But his diligence and example, was noted by the authority,
Selecting him to a position of trust—and appointed him chief trustee.

So Joseph had free access to each and every cell,
The prisoners grew to like him, and confided in him as well.
One day on his rounds, while he was issuing out the food,

He noticed the butler and baker's faces in a solem mood.
"What ails you fellows, and what makes you look so sad?
If I can help in anyway, I'll only be too glad."

"We've both been dreaming," the butler said. "Strange unusual dreams.
And what is most distressing, there's no one to interpret . . . so it seems."
"Don't worry, men," Joseph said, with a kind of smile.
"I used to dream myself once, but I haven't for a while.
God can give the meaning—so tell your dreams to me.
Which one's going to start first? . . . You, butler, how'd that be?"

The butler's dream was of three branches on a single vine.
Which budded, blossomed, and bore clusters of fruit.
Taking the fruit into his hand, the butler squeezed it into Pharoah's cup,
Then passed it on to Pharaoh, for him to have a sup.

"That's a very good dream," Joseph revealed, "for the three branches,
Represent three days (and Pharoah has had time to meditate).
And your passing him the cup, after three days; he will you reinstate.
You'll get your job back, that is true; for Pharaoh has forgiven you."

"Thank you, Joseph—thank you much. I'll repay you one day, you can trust . . . "
"All right, butler—just remember me, when you're back at work again,
For I'll be still a prisoner—unless I'm freed—and that is very plain."

"Now it's my turn," the baker said eagerly. "Here's my dream,
    that I dreamt—
For you to reveal to me. I was carrying three baskets,
Loaded with good things to eat. They were positioned on my
    head—
Birds flying all around—so neat. Then the birds swooped down
    on me,
And picked at the top-most basket. Why they did this I don't
    know,
But they did eat greedily."

"Now, this meaning is not so good, baker," said Joseph solemnly.
"The three baskets are also three days, when Pharaoh reviews
    your case.
You will be taken out of here, but the outcome's not good for
    you—I fear—
The birds that were picking at your head—means you'll be
    hung—until you're dead."

The dreams came true as Joseph had already predicted.
In three days' time, the butler to his old job returned
And the baker taken out, and executed.
(There is a thought here, that tends to puzzle me—
If Joseph had interpreted the baker's dream first,
How eager do you think the butler would be?)

Continuing the drudgery of prison life, Joseph was still out on a
    limb.
But days grew into weeks, and weeks into months
Until two whole years went by before the butler remembered
    him.

For Pharaoh (the ruler) had had a dream,
Which none of the magicians or wise men could tell.
Pharaoh was distraught—and his temper was rising as well.
Then the butler remembered Joseph—then he ventured to say,
"If it please my master, whilst I was in prison, I met a Hebrew man—
I'd had a dream, which he interpreted—and he did it well!
So if anyone can help you, I'm sure that Joseph is the man."

"Send for Joseph," Pharaoh said, "Send for the Hebrew prisoner."
The words echoed through the court rooms—and to the prison gate.
Joseph was summoned before Pharaoh, thinking what would be his fate?
He bathed, shaved, and to him was a new set of clothes given.
Then out of the prison surrounds he stepped—
And breathed the fresh air of heaven.

Joseph Rises to Fame

Pharaoh looked at Joseph, saying, "You can interpret dreams!
I've heard tell. These are my dreams that are troubling me.
I want you to interpret them well!"
"I am not able to interpret dreams," said Joseph, as he spoke out,
 quite bold.
"But, my God in heaven—through me—will give you your
 answer.
And I'll tell you what I am told."

The first dream that Pharaoh had had was of cattle by the Nile.
They were fat and sleek beasts, numbering seven—no more.
They were feeding by the reeds—then up came seven more,
And they were thin and gaunt of figure,
Which then ate up the seven fat kine, and after eating
 them—were no bigger,
Being still as thin and gaunt as they were before.

Pharaoh then turned over and went to sleep again
And very soon he was dreaming—this time of ears of grain,
Seven good and full ears upon a single stalk—
Then seven withered thin and blighted ears appeared.
And swallowed up the good and full ears.

Joseph informed Pharaoh that although the dreams were
 different, both dreams
Were one—the doubling of the dream, had been fixed by God—
His seal upon the prophecy, and upon what was to be done.
Both the seven good cattle, and the seven good ears, represented
 seven good years.
Seven years of good harvest followed by seven years of famine,
Which were portrayed by the thin cattle, and ears the same.

Joseph continued and advised to appoint a supply officer
Who could conserve the surplus in the years of plenty
And to be issued out by him, during the famine—when their cupboards were empty.

Pondering with careful thought, Pharaoh looked on Joseph, as he ought.
"You've planted an idea, within my head. I'll make you my supply officer.
Let it be so, for I have said I'm promoting you in this land,
Making you second under my command.
You will be ruler in all but name." And that's how Joseph rose to fame.
God had blessed him—as he always says,
Those who are faithful, and will follow His ways.

Joseph's fame was known both from near and far,
He was even given an Egyptian name—Za-phen Nath Pane ah.
Life was good, with plenty of work to be done, and it was grand.
He organized building programs in many of the towns,
For storage places were required—right throughout the land.
Trade was booming—everything going swell—full employment,
And with bumper harvests the granaries began to fill.

Joseph was established, and decided to take the marriage path.
He married the daughter of a priest of On—whose name was As-en-ath.
The marriage was blessed by their firstborn son.
So Manasseh their son, was given, to Joseph, and his spouse.
(For Joseph said, "God's made me forget all my hardships, and all my father's house.")

A second son was born to them, Ephraim—a boy of great
    perfection
(For God had made Joseph fruitful in the land of his affliction.)
However prosperous Joseph had become, with his instant rise to
    fame.
What would seem profit to most—to him was a contradiction,
For he still considered Egypt was the land of his affliction.

As Joseph had predicted, the prophecy in the dreams, had come
    true.
They'd had years of plenty; now the lean years had approached
    them too.
All the lands round Egypt were all in dire distress,
For they had, not had the foresight, which God had endowed
    Joseph with.
They had not provided—and times were very hard—
And without food and sustenance, all they could do was starve.

Conditions were the same in Canaan, where Jacob, and his
    family lived.
And Jacob talking to his sons said, "Why are you standing
    looking at each other,
While the children are starving, as well as your mother?
The traders say as they passed that way, that there's corn in
    Egypt yet.
Pack your mules, and on your way, and see what you can get.
All of you go, but the youngest—Benjamin—stays at home
Under my care. I've lost one son already and that's too much to
    bear!"

And so the brothers loaded up—ten of them in all.
And set out, with their mules, not knowing what would befall.
Egypt was far away, but when hunger is the master,
You'll drive your mules and yourself, to go a little faster.

Joseph Reunited with His Family

"So this is Egypt," said Simeon to Reuben, his elder brother,
"It might be a good place to live if you had no other."
Reuben nodded his head, and then he said, "I've heard it's a land of fame.
But we're not here as sightseers—we've come to buy some grain."

So to the governor's house, they found their way, bowing as they entered.
Not knowing the language, it was hard to say, just what they had intended.
Joseph the governor knew them—he knew them straightaway.
He was rough to them—in his pretence—as through an interpreter, he did say.
"If you don't want grain, you're not hungry men." Then he raised his eyes.
"I do believe that you've come here, as a bunch of spies.
You've come to spy out our land, to find its weakest spot.
Your empty bags, and mule train is camouflage—tell me if it's not?"

The brothers they were all concerned, and bowed and bowed again.
"We are not spies, your honour, we've come here to purchase grain."
Joseph sighed, as he watched his brothers—sighed, and he knew,
That the dreams that God had given to him had at last come true.

"We are not spies, your honour," they spoke out once again.
"We are all sons of one man—Jacob is his name.
We were twelve to start with, but one is no more—and the youngest
Had to stay at home, for our father's word is law."

Joseph outwardly seemed unconvinced, saying, "I will test you then,
You'll all be detained, but one man, who'll return and bring your brother back again."
The brothers went into conference, and they were unaware,
That Joseph could understand them, for he spoke through an interpreter.
They said how they'd wronged their brother, and remembered his look of distress,
As they sold him to Ishmaelite traders—a look they'd never forget.
And now because of their past sin, God was judging so they could not win.
The time had come, they'd have to pay for what happened on that day.

Joseph withdrew, for he could not stand, and listen to their woe.
In another room, where none could see, he let the tears flow,
For he loved his brethren in his heart, but he would not tell them so.
And for three days he placed them all in prison—then he
Reversed his first decision, saying all of them could go, save one.
Then to their surprise, he bound Simeon up right before their eyes.
The rest could go, he told them. They were loaded up with grain.
"Remember to return with your brother, or you won't see my face again."

The nine brothers returned to Canaan, and when each one
 opened up his sack,
He found his money securely tied; right there within the pack.
They could not understand it, for each had tendered his money.
It must be a trap of some kind, and that wasn't very funny.

When they told their tale to their father, Jacob was distraught,
He said, "Joseph is no more, Simeon is no more, and now you
 ask
To take Benjamin from me. What am I being taught?
You'll not take him, and that's final. We'll all starve first, you
 see."
(But when hunger is the master, bold words strike emptily.)

Once all their food was nearly gone, Jacob said to his sons once
 more,
"Off you go and load your mules—and to Egypt go again,
Buy what you can, in quantity, for we need the grain."
Judah spoke up and said, "It's useless to try again. Unless
We take our Benjamin, we'll not get any grain,
For that man was most emphatic, for he told us, and told us quite
 plain.
'If you do not bring your brother, you'll not see my face again.' "

Reuben had also assured his dad, that he would responsible be,
And should he not return with the lad, "then my own two sons,
You may take from me." Judah strengthened the statement
By adding his further persuasion that if they did not go at once,
They'd all die of starvation.

Jacob reluctantly agreed, then said, "Take the governor some
 local fruit—
Nuts and other gifts—Oh! and double the money that he asks—
Because of the cash found in your sacks. You're all packed,

So off you go. It could have been an oversight, you know."
Jacob watched them go out of sight, then prayed with all his might,
That God would keep them safe on their journey—and grant them mercy,
As He can—when they would stand before that man!

When Joseph learned that the brothers had arrived, and that Benjamin was with them—
And so soon! He bade his servants to prepare a feast,
For they were to eat with him at noon.
When the brothers were told that they to the governor's house must go,
They were both hesitant and reluctant, and their going was very slow.
Thinking that the money in their sacks, was judged as having been stolen;
They tried to put on a brave face, and their countenances embolden.
They told Joseph's steward their story, about the cash in their packs.
The steward nodded knowingly and said, "It's very odd. Perhaps the treasure
In the sacks—eh! Perhaps it was from God."

The cautious brothers bowed very low, as Joseph entered the room.
With a hasty glance, he saw Benjamin was there—then his heart pounded.
As he quickly dropped his stir, he enquired about their dad;
And was relieved on finding out that his father was alive and well.
He had to curb a jubilant shout. He glanced again at Benjamin—

Then quickly left the room before his emotions got the better of him,
Giving his secret away too soon.

Groups of people sat down to eat, according to their rank and station.
As Egyptians would not be seated by any of the Hebrew nation.
They looked on them as inferior and would have called it an abomination.
The brothers were served from Joseph's table, they had all that they could eat.
But Benjamin's helping was large—five times as large—and that was no mean feat.
After the meal, Joseph told his steward to fill his brother's sacks with grain:
Also to include their money—with his own drinking cup to be placed
In Benjamin's sack—then to tie them all up again.

The brothers started on their return journey, each congratulating himself.
How easy it had all been; so why had they feared in Egypt—this land of wealth.
They hadn't gone very far, when a messenger ran and stopped them;
Asking why they were returning evil for good, for the governor's cup,
His own silver cup, had disappeared —and must be with them.
The brothers were indignant, but agreed that the culprit must be punished;
Offering themselves to become Joseph's slaves, but the judgement was to be
Reserved for the wrongdoer, whoever that might be.

When the sacks were opened, the silver cup was found.
Hidden in the bottom of Benjamin's sack—right there near the ground.
They just could not believe it—just what could they say,
Looking at each other in a dismal downcast way
So they all about-turned, and went to the governor's home,
And to await his justice, allotted to the youngest one.

Judah became the advocate; he outlined the story well.
He told Joseph of famine, hunger, and the journey they had to take.
They'd been forced to relate personal matters, of the family in Canaan,
About their father and youngest brother, whose name is Benjamin.
Then Joseph had detained Simeon until they returned with their brother
Much to their father's reluctance, but they couldn't do any other.
And that, just so Joseph could look at him—to prove
That none of them, was a spy. . . . If they returned without the youngest boy,
He felt that their father would die,
For Benjamin was the only surviving son—of his father's favourite wife.
Judah completed by saying, "Forgive the lad. Take me into bondage,
And I'll be your slave for life."

Joseph could contain himself no longer; he wept aloud, quite deeply—
Then dismissing the servants—revealed himself to his brothers,
Greeting each one with mixed emotion, and feelings—
Lots of joy, midst great floods of tears.

Joseph then told his brothers not to be angry, or distressed,
For he had heard them, when they confessed.
True, they had sold him into Egypt, but it was not of man.
It was according to God's plan to preserve life.
And Joseph had been used in that plan—two years of famine
Had gone by, leaving five to go—when no ploughing or harvest would take place.
God had made Joseph a father to Pharaoh, in a plan to save the human race.

When Joseph had composed himself, he then hastened on his brothers.
"Hurry, go and tell my father, the good news (and of course, the others)
That God has made me lord over all Egypt, and that all of you,
Can dwell in this land—that's all the family—in an area called Goshen—
And God will provide for you, and He will do it . . . through me.
Tell Father about Egypt, its buildings, pomp and splendour.
You'll all be welcome—I know you will—you just wait and see.
For Pharaoh's even providing wagons, to help you, on your journey."

So they were all reunited—a great big family.
They had grown from just a few, now numbering seventy.
Their story is not over, but it's the end of this episode.
They eventually left Egypt, but by a different road.

We hope you liked these few verses—perhaps you thought them grand.
But one thing we must remember—Egypt is Egypt.
And not the promised land.

Pharaoh and the Plagues of Egypt

Pharaoh was a hard king, hard on all the Jews;
If ever they asked a favour, he'd listen; then refuse.
He considered them beneath him, only fit to labour on;
They'd been eased into the position of slavery, by those, who worshiped the sun.

He did not know of Joseph, or at least, pretended so,
The one who had saved Egypt from starvation, and caused Egypt's wealth, to grow.
Joseph's management, had been an inspiration; he'd been placed in a position of
Trust, selling corn to all the nations, causing Egypt's treasury to swell, and almost burst,
But that King had long passed on, and another Pharaoh, was on the throne,
Who accepted all the wealth his benefactor had brought him,
But his family, he did, disown.
True they brought him wealth—as slavery, was profitable—of course;
And Pharaoh himself was without remorse, and Egypt was set for years to come,
On a vast building program, and an even vaster, labour force.

The Hebrew slaves worked hard, theirs a thankless task.
They made bricks from morn till dusk, no time to lounge, or bask.
Many a back was bleeding, by stripes from the overseer's whip,
"Hurry up, you Hebrews, stop idling, increase your pace, and quick!"
Petitions were made to the taskmaster, to ease their aching limbs.
But often a snarl, was his reply, "If they worked harder, they wouldn't feel their pains,

They get fed, they sleep at night, they even get washed, when it rains:
They've had it far too easy, we even provide the straw."
Then a gleam came into Pharaoh's eye. "But in the future, we won't, not any more.
They'll gather their own straw from now on," then he added with a frown,
"And I'll flog the slave, with all my might, if I find his quota down."

Moses had been chosen by God, to deliver Israel from their plight.
He tried hard, to avoid the fight, saying. "You know, Lord, that I stutter."
So his brother, Aaron, was appointed spokesman, and given the words to utter.
They cautiously entered the palace (to Moses, it was familiar ground).
The court was lined, with Pharaoh's magicians, but no friendly face, to be found.

Now Pharaoh accepted Moses as a god, and Aaron as his mouthpiece.
So Pharaoh listened, to their petition, but he was not impressed.
Why should the whole Hebrew nation, want to go to the wilderness?
Just to worship their God, so that, they could be blessed?
The Egyptians didn't do it, so why should they?
It was but an excuse for laziness, just to idle, their time away.
Surely, Egypt was a big enough place, in which to worship.
The Egyptians did it—so why not they?

Following God's direction, Aaron's rod was thrown on the ground,
That rod became a writhing serpent, but Pharaoh was not impressed.
He just puckered up his lips, and nodded to his magicians, standing around.
They in turn threw down their rods, and soon on the palace floor,
Was a writhing mass of serpents; but quickly reduced to one:
For Aaron's serpent just swallowed theirs, which resulted in stopping their fun.
But Pharaoh's heart was hardened, he would not let them go.
No matter how Moses and Aaron pleaded, Pharaoh just answered, "No!"

Moses and Aaron rose up early, for such was the bidding of God.
They made their way to the Nile bank, taking with them Aaron's rod.
They waited Pharaoh's arrival, and said, "Let my people go."
Pharaoh rubbed his sleep-filled eyes and shook his head, saying, "No!"
So Aaron's rod was lifted up, and he smote the river Nile.
The waters they became as blood, and the fish died, after a while.

The smell became offensive, so Pharaoh declined to bathe,
Until channels were dug on the river bank, just like a shallow grave,
Into which, the filtered water seeped, barely enough to shave.
Pharaoh looked to his wise men, looked for their support;
And they too, made water to be as blood, and making room for thought.
So Pharaoh's heart was hard, and would not let the people go.
"On with your work, you slaves, and increase your pace from slow."

The next plague that came about, was when Aaron stretched
    forth his hand.
Frogs seemed to come out from nowhere, covering all the land.
Pharaoh called to his magicians, and they did the same.
They produced frogs all right, but could not make them go, again.
Pharaoh was distraught, frogs were everywhere, in the kitchen,
In the dough trough, even on his chair—in the bedrooms.

On the beds, they went hopping there; whether you walked,
Or whether you sat: you would hear a squelch, their cold wet,
    clammy bodies,
Were adorning, many a palace shelf.
The drains were blocked with corpses, you couldn't clean the
    floor,
For as you moved, say ten or so, they were replaced, by a dozen
    more.

In desperation, Pharaoh pleaded with Moses, to take the frogs
    away.
"Entreat, the Lord your God, to take the frogs away; and then
The Hebrew nation can be up, and on their way."
Moses replied to Pharaoh, "Just when, would you like the frogs
    to go?"
Pharaoh thought and pulled his beard, and said, "Tomorrow, we'll
Put up with them today." The frogs they died one and all,
But, oh! The awful smell, you had to wear a mask,
And boil the water from the well.

When Pharaoh saw, that there was relief, his heart, became hard
    again,
Saying, "The children of Israel cannot go, they're all my slaves,
    and that's quite plain."

"If my people cannot go," said Moses, "There's another plague for you."
And Aaron's rod struck the ground. The dust became lice, that's true.
The itching courtiers, tried to look at ease, but secretly scratched their backs and knees.
Till Pharaoh openly scratched his head, and gave his beard a shake.
"Come on, magicians, do your stuff, what do you think, I pay you for?"
The magicians tried hard, without success, as Pharaoh scratched some more.
The wise men looked at Pharaoh, and declared, "This is the finger of God.
You'd be wise to listen to Moses—and to heed, his servant's rod."
But Pharaoh was the ruler, he was monarch there.
He made all the decisions, and now that the plagues, had cleared the air.
"No, my slaves won't go. I've told you from the start, they're my slaves
As you all know, and I suffer, from the hardness of heart."

The next plague that followed, was that of flies, blood-sucking, gadflies,
But as Moses had predicted, it was the land of Egypt that was afflicted.
The land of Goshen, it was free. God had made a division, between his people
And the enemy, and that was very clear, as everyone could see.
The Egyptians could not move, for flies—biting, and sucking, their blood.

If they walked, or if they ran, or covered their faces with a hood;
Those pinching, sucking, bloodthirsty insects, found a spot to bite:
And bite they did, as if starving, and blood, was their delight.
"Take them away," Pharaoh shouted. "Your people can have their way,
Your people they can sacrifice, I promise you," and the plague, was taken away.
But Pharaoh's heart grew harder, so in Egypt, they had to stay.

The next woe that followed, was upon the Egyptian cattle.
Pharaoh's larder, was depleting, as the Egyptian cattle died.
But the Hebrew cattle, they just thrived, and lived, and multiplied.
God had divided once again, between His people, and those in the world.
But Pharaoh was a stubborn man; he'd relent under pressure, then change,
Alter his tune, as the pressure eased, and with a frown on face, say,
"No, why should I let my slaves go? No, I won't! No, no, no!"

The slaves, were slaves, and bricks were being made, and the busy furnace
Accumulated lots of ash, a by-product of that trade.
So Moses went to the furnace, and taking handfuls of ash.
Sprinkled it towards heaven, right there in Pharaoh's sight.
Pharaoh looked on in amusement, thinking, *What could he be doing now?*
Is this a form of sacrifice? Queer people, trying to escape somehow.
But his amusement, gave way to jabs of pain, as he tried to walk away.

He was suffering, from boils and blains, his face changed to dismay.
He surveyed his courtiers, trying to look at ease.
One fellow (while actually bowing), was giving a boil a squeeze.
They could neither sit, nor stand, and lying down, was a bed of pain.
I'll let them go, thought Pharaoh, *I'll not lie again.*
Good riddance to them, I'll be bound, Oh, to be free from pain.
Even the cattle are suffering, when can I sit down, again?
At last the plague was lifted, but the Lord hardened Pharaoh's heart.
He should have let the Hebrews go, right from the very start.

Now Moses came with a warning, to remove all cattle indoors,
For another plague was on its way—that of thunder, hail, and fire;
And the Egyptian cattle not moved indoors—were lying down dead in the mire.
They had been killed, by the hailstones—really large, chunks of ice.
They had fallen in a deluge, breaking the trees, as they fell.
The thunder was truly deafening, and the fire, a reminder of hell.
But all this, was in Egyptians' land, they were the ones, being judged.
While in Goshen all was pleasant, their cattle had not even budged.
God looks after his people, protects them, one and all.
He cares for those who love Him, and lifts them, should they fall.

Pharaoh humbled himself, before Moses, confessing his faults that day.
He would let the people go, why should he longer delay?
Then when the plague had ceased, Pharaoh was heard to say,
"Why should I let my slaves go? They are my very own,

If I let my slaves go, they never will return, back home."
Then a smile smirked, on his cunning face, "I'll let all the men go:
They can sacrifice, and worship, then they will return—I know!"

But the men, did not go alone, and another plague followed on,
This time God sent locusts, blocking out the light of the sun.
They came along in millions, devouring all things green,
Anything left by the plague of hail, was now, nowhere to be seen.
The clouds of locust hovered, and possessed the land,
Devouring all the green growth, leaving only sand.
You'd think, that Pharaoh would have softened, when a famine
Was about to start. But this time, Pharaoh had no choice;
For God had hardened his heart.

The ninth plague it was darkness, darkness throughout the land.
All Egypt was in darkness; it was a depth of darkness—touchable by hand.
It was so intense that it could be felt, and only the blind, could see.
But as for the land of Goshen, no darkness; it was light and free.
The blackness lasted for three days, and Pharaoh said, "Enough's enough.
You and your families, can go, but your cattle stay, and that for you, may be tough."
Moses then answered wise, "No, we, our families, and cattle go, we'll not compromise."

Pharaoh was mad at Moses, angrier than at the start.
For God was dealing with Pharaoh, and had hardened his heart.
God was passing judgement, upon the Egyptian race,
For their sins and wickedness, and treatment of His chosen race.

One more plague was yet to come, before the slaves went free,
The Egyptians, looking at the Hebrew homes, were amazed, at what they could see.
The husband with a bowl of blood, and a branch from a hyssop tree,
Painting door posts and lintels, working away, so busily.
Bags were packed, bundles tied with rope, carts loaded, prepared for a journey.

The Egyptians shook their heads, as if showing sympathy.
"They are a peculiar people, just look at the way they act,
They've even borrowed gold, silver, and jewels, and some clothing too from me,
When they knocked and asked, we felt sorry, and gave them liberally."

But for the Egyptians, true sorrow was yet to come; it came after all the warnings.
For on that night, the Angel of Death arrived, taking the first-born of man and beast.
All those, not covered by the blood, from the highest to the least.
A cry went out, over all the land, wails and laments, from far and near,
Anguish and grief, pitiful sobs, deep heart-felt weeping, and shaking all over with fear.
Such is the Lord's judgement, if you will not hear!

Excitement and anticipation, were seen in the Hebrew camp, and at last, they understood.
They had eaten, and were ready, and ready for a hasty move.
The Angel of Death, had passed over, and they were covered by the blood.
They gathered together in families, each within his tribe.
They followed Moses, he as their leader, and he would be their guide.

Egyptian soldiers, were hovering around, bidding them make haste.
Pharaoh wanted to see the back of them, he'd had more than a taste.
The Children of Israel were on the move, not one of them sick or lame;
For the Lord God took care of them, and He's every day, the same.

The Red Sea, was a barrier, but no obstacle to God,
For Moses stood upon the shore, and he raised Aaron's rod.
The waters parted left and right, giving them a highway through it.
But before they reached the other side, the faint-hearted, began to rue it.

For there in the distance behind them, and rapidly gaining ground,
Were Pharaoh and his army, riding in furious haste; he was trying to regain his losses,
With his chariots and fighting men;
But what had been a highway, became a soggy, and marshy ground.
Wheels came off the chariots, horses slipped and fell, and were lying all around,
For when you have God fighting for you, you can smile at the efforts of men.
For on God's side, you're a conqueror, you can prove it, again and again.

When the Children of Israel crossed over, and were safe on the other side,
Moses raised Aaron's rod again, the parted waters united, and then flowed on
With the flowing tide; taking with it Pharaoh's army, chariots and horses as well,
For they were all dead and drowned, with not one of them left, to tell.

So why be like the Egyptians, living constantly in the land of sin?
Why try to fight, for what you know's not right, and you know you cannot win?
Why not be on God's side; the side of right and good?
Remember Jesus is our atonement; for you He shed His blood.
You can have salvation, through just believing—eternal life assured.
Live a life that's full and free, then collect your reward.

Gideon

Gideon was by the winepress, and he was threshing grain.
He'd stop, he'd pause, and listen, then he'd thresh again.
There were strong reasons for his caution, and why, he was out of sight,
For the enemy was within earshot, showing off their might.

Israel had done evil, and was being judged for their sin.
For they followed after Amorite gods, had groves, and worshiped there within.
Now for seven years, Midian had dominated them, and was now joined by
The armies of the children of the East, and of the Amalekites.
They had laid siege, against Israel, using up all their food.
They came with cattle, and camels, tramping down their crops,
Not doing them any good: they came in droves with staves. They appeared like
Grasshoppers; Israel fled before them, and dwelt in dens, and caves.

Under the oak at Ophrah, an angel appeared to Gideon, and gave him the
Following greeting: "The Lord is with thee, thou mighty man of valour."
Gideon was at first, speechless, then queried the greeting.
But the angel continued, saying, "Go in this, thy might.
And thou shall save Israel, from the hand of the Midianite."

Gideon stammered, "But my family is poor in Manasseh,
And I am but the least." Nevertheless he obeyed.
He made a sacrifice, upon a rock, with a kid, unleavened cakes,

And poured over them a broth. The angel touched them with his staff,
And fire immediately consumed them.

The miracle impressed him. It set his heart aflame.
The angel had called him mighty; he must live up to that name.
He took the seven-year-old bullock, and with him ten other men.
They pulled down the heathen altars, and cut down the groves, beside them.

Then Gideon sacrificed his bullock, using the wood as fuel.
The locals—they were furious; they thought his deed most cruel.
They demanded that Joash (Gideon's father), surrender his son to be killed.
But Joash stood there, by his son, saying, "Not one drop of his blood to be spilled."
And he decried the heathen worshipers, and their gods.
Now the Midianites, Amalekites, and the children of the East armies,
Were encamped in the valley of Jezreel.
Gideon sent messengers to Asher, Zebulun, and Naphtali, asking them to join him,
And strong, was his appeal, for many came to join him.

Although Gideon had had a message, he wanted to make sure.
So out, he put a fleece, and prayed, that the fleece it would be wet,
And all around be dry, if he was in the will of God.
God answered him, for the fleece was wet, and yet
All the ground was dry.

He asked God to forgive him, but he'd like another try,
That all the ground be wet, and that the fleece it would be dry.
By confirmation, God answered him, and Gideon, at last was sure,
That he would triumph, in the cause, for God's word, is pure.

Gideon's call had been answered by twenty-two thousand men,
But they're too many, he was informed, so he sent the fearful, home again.
There still remained ten thousand, some of them he must erase,
Or man would take the credit—and not give God the praise.

So a test was implemented, to the water they had to go.
All were to drink by their own choice, and their drinking habits would show,
Which of them were chosen, and which were counted out.
The majority knelt down to drink, while a few lapped hand to mouth.
The few, they were selected, three hundred chosen men.
They had to do Gideon's bidding, and he would tell them when.

Gideon was still apprehensive, of what the outcome might be.
So he took Phurah, his servant, with him, and headed to the enemy.
They listened, at the unguarded tents, to learn of their morale.
One was telling of a dream he'd had, of a cake of barley bread.
It tumbled into the Midian camp, and overturned a tent, he said.
An interpreter said it means, that Gideon would deliver them.
Now Gideon was delighted—and returned his thanks to God.
His heavy heart was lightened—as back to the others he trod.

Gideon divided up his group into three separate parts, one hundred men in
Each, and each man to have a trumpet, pitcher, and a lamp—the lighted lamps
Were to be placed within the pitchers, and carried around the camp.
The three groups formed up, in separate lines on the hill of Moreh,
Over the enemy, in the camp below, the given signal, came quite clear.
They smashed their pitchers, then their trumpets began to blow.
They raised their lamps, and with a mighty noise, shouted to those below,
"The sword of the Lord, and of Gideon."
The enemy host were startled, they ran, they cried, they fled.
As the three hundred trumpets were blown so loudly. The following it is said:
"That the Lord set every man's sword, against his fellow."
They slew each other, as they took flight, closely chased
By the Israelites—Israel stepping out with giant strides.
Victoriously they took the fords, they captured two princes, Zeeb and Oreb,
Slaying them in the winepress, and cutting off each head.

The grateful Israelis, were now freed, from their enemies' yoke.
They asked Gideon to be their ruler; he thought, and then he spoke.
"Thank you, for your confidence. It's good of you to ask;
God, He gave me a mission, and I've fulfilled that task,
I'd prefer to settle down, and live in my own home."

And settle down he really did, he was never out of funds,
For he married, many wives, and fathered seventy sons.
So God, through Gideon, gave Israel their release,
And for the next forty years, they could sleep in peace.

David the Shepherd

David was a shepherd boy, who looked after his father's sheep.
A responsible job for one who cared, not one for the mild and meek.
He spent many peaceful hours, playing on his shepherd's pipe—or just practising
With his sling—then at other times—he'd just lie on his back,
Look up to the sky, and blissfully sing.

He enjoyed those peaceful times, for he could commune with God.
He saw God in all creation. He knew that the Lord was his Shepherd,
Which caused him much elation.

But all days were not so peaceful—ofttimes, danger would occur.
One time it was a lion—and another time a bear.
They were after the sheep, as an instant meal,
But the watchful shepherd was there,
For he killed the lion, and he killed the bear.
Some said that David was a good shot—and the tale was quite a story.
But David knew that God directed those shots and gave Him all the glory.

One day at home, his father, Jesse, said to him, "Your brothers, are all up
On the fighting line—guarding our frontiers. Take this food and drink to them,
It may help to quell their fears,
For the enemy is spread out in bold array, shouting threats, and insults,

Daring Israel to present a champion, to match their giant Goliath."

When David arrived at the front, it was as his father had told.
The Israeli troops were quaking, not one of them very bold.
He enquired of his brothers, "Why are we all so afraid of Philistines?"
"Have you seen their giant?" they screamed. "The ground trembles as he walks past.
He's threatened us for days, saying this day will be our last.
He's thrown out an ultimatum, to match him, or admit defeat.
And no one's brave enough to try; just look at the size of his feet."

"If no one will go, then I will," said David to his brothers.
"Don't talk rot, shepherd boy; away, and mind your sheep.
Leave the fighting to those who are trained, not amateurs, or others."

David went up to the king's tent, and found King Saul, very sad.
"I've come to offer my services," said the shepherd lad.
"But, you're only a boy; just look at your small size.
Their giant's over nine feet tall, you'd hardly come up to his thighs."

"I have the Lord with me;" David said. "He's helped me many a day;
He helped me once to kill a bear, then a lion He helped me slay."
"All right," said the king. "Put my armour on—you'll need protection from him,
Or your chances will be very slim."
David had Saul's armour on, but had to struggle to walk,
For Saul himself was a tall man, head and shoulders above his clan.

"It can't be done, Your Majesty," said David as he shuffled back.
"I'd never get there in this suit, though I try with all my might.
I can hardly move my arms, let alone raise them to fight."
Once out of the armour, David breathed—he breathed a sigh of relief.
What a burden for a fighting man; he was glad he looked after sheep.

On the way to the battle front, he stopped awhile at the brook;
Carefully selecting the stones, and five of them he took.
His selection was careful, and calculated, for it was smooth stones that he chose,
So their flight would be accurate, without sharp edges, to impose.
The number five had a meaning also, for there are five letters in a word named faith,
And David was going forth, in faith, faith in God, to prevail.

Goliath, he was angry, when he saw young David approach.
All he could see was a shepherd boy, and in his hand a sling.
"Am I a dog?" he roared, "that you come at me with stones and a sling.
Where are the fighting men of Israel? All crouching in their cave!
They send a lad with stones; what honour can he save?"

He thumped the ground with his heavy feet, roaring as he threw out his threats.
But David calmly selected a stone, and placed it in his sling, then boldly
Announced for all to hear, "I come in the Name of the Lord God."
As he drew near, he slung the sling, and released the stone;
It flew really accurately, for God's guidance it was there, the stone flew

Through the air, striking the giant full and square.
Right between the eyes it struck him—he fell headlong to the ground.
David rushed up, grasping the giant's own sword, and cut off the giant's head.

The watching troops on both sides shouted at the turn of events:
The Philistines shouted in dismay, as down their champion went.
The Israelis on the other hand, they let up a cheer,
And gave their feelings vent, as they hastened to pursue
Their enemy, who were retreating in disarray,
For God had given them the victory.
Through Him, they had won the day.

We have a lot to learn from this story, a story of faith in action
David had faith in God's deliverance, which was a great deal more, than a fraction.
For as he stepped out, with his battle shout;
The angry giant was all in a rage, he'd lost his temper, but that's not all.
David's calmness and faith, was his downfall. So once again, let it be said,
Step out in faith, keep calm; it's the enemy, who will lose his head.

Esther

Now Vashti was a naughty girl, even though she was the queen,
For Ahasueras the king, had called her to him, so that she could be seen.
Now Ahasueras was a mighty king, and ruled the Persian empire—
It was a massive area and stretched from India to Ethiopia.
It covered over 127 provinces. Ahasueras made a feast, inviting all the princes.
The feast in Shushan was a big one—and lasted half a year.

It was during that time, that Vashti the queen, also had a feast,
And invited all the ladies; they talked, and talked, and talked some more;
Until it reached a peak. It went on from day to day, lasting, a whole week.

One day the king, who was making merry, for he had been drinking wine,
Called to his chamberlains, "Go, bring the queen, for I wish to boast, what's mine."
Now the queen had been talking, talking, talking—to all her ladies.
"What does the king want now, I wonder? I don't think I'll go and see.
He may rule this empire, that's for sure, but I draw the line with me.
You know, girls, we should stand together—the men have all the say.
We're the ones who need liberating—let's start with this today!"
(But those in positions of authority should also bow and bend;
For their positions demand example, and not to start a trend).

So rebellion had raised its head; she scorned His Majesty;
The king went pale, then angry; he could not understand Vashti.
He consulted his advisers, asking what action, they should take.
They thought, and talked it over, of the decision they had to make.
"If you, O king, who rules this land, have your authority undermined,
You've no option, but to replace your queen, replace her, with another kind.
For you have been attacked, and it's only a matter of time,
For that abuse, of authority—to trickle down the line . . . "

The king nodded in agreement. "We must make a show of force.
I will denounce Vashti as my queen; I'll give her a bill of divorce.
So now go—go through all the land, and choose a suitable bride for me;
Let her be loving, obedient, kind—the opposite of Vashti."

So Vashti was divorced, and stripped of all her glory;
That was not the end of course; so now hear this story.
Now, amongst the maidens selected as the prospective, future bride,
Was a Jewish girl named Esther, whom her ancestry, she did hide.
For she had neither father or mother, but a relative—her cousin Mordecai,
Who treated her—as his very own child.
He had advised her, when entering the bride contest.
To hide her nationality, or the anti-Jewish element would certainly protest.

The preparation for selection was quite a lengthy one;
Two different periods of six months; the first one with oil of myrrh.

The second consisted of treatment, with spices of sweet odour.
The king's chamberlain, Hegai, was the overseer of all the candidates,
And he favoured Esther as the winner, for he didn't know her creed.
He favoured her right from the start, supplying her every need.
His judgement was right, as it had always been,
For Esther was chosen—and she became the queen.

During this time Mordecai would daily attend at the king's gate
To listen to the latest news, any gossip from the palace,
And the welcome of the king's new mate.
It was at this period, that he overheard two of the chamberlains,
Bigthan and Teresh, who were doorkeepers, planning and whispering a word.
Their plans were to lay hands on the king, his royal majesty.
Now Mordecai reported this terrible scheme to Esther, relating the whole story.

Queen Esther reported the proposed plan to the right authority;
It was truly recorded in the chronicles of His Majesty.
The villains, they were questioned, found guilty, and hanged upon a tree.

It was about this time that Haman, found favour with the king,
And Ahasueras promoted him, high above those in court.
And Haman's pride just swelled and swelled, as he thought, it ought.
The order went out to do Haman the honour due.
For all to stand as he approached, then bow low, as if to tie a shoe.
Haman strutted as he went, with amazing dignity; his elevated pride, it showed
What his inner thoughts must be, but as he passed the king's gate,

His pride suffered a rebuff, for Mordecai just sat there, and
    looked at him,
And that was more than enough. He'd always hated Jews—
For they were the conquered race; they were there under
    sufferance.
He tried to ignore the noncompliance, then increased his pace.

When Haman arrived home, his face portrayed what he thought.
His wife asked if he were sick—or something of the sort.
"It's not me who's sickening, but those infernal Jews.
They're in every profitable corner—they're up to every ruse;
And now today, as I left the court, there sat one of them,
Simply glaring at me, as if, I were him—and that he, was me!
It took me all my inner strength, to preserve my dignity.
Oh! These Jews will drive me up the wall, and that one,
    Mordecai, he's the worst of all."

"Now, now dear," said Zeresh, his wife, "you just calm down,
For the upset, will do your blood pressure strife.
You are far too clever a man—to be outsmarted by one of the
    Jewish race,
Especially that Mordecai man. Just think hard—you'll find a
    plan.
To remove your stumbling block; you're the king's
    favourite—his right-hand man.
You're in a position to give those Jews a very nasty shock."
Haman's face, slowly showed a very cunning smile.
"You are so right, my dear; you have so much wisdom and care,
Beneath your lovely head of hair."

Haman devised a plan, and brought it before the king.
"You know, O King," he said, "there is a people in this land,
Scattered far and wide; they disregard your laws, and their
    contempt

They do not hide—and they're more trouble, than they're worth,
And I myself will offer ten thousand talents of silver—in payment
For their extermination. They are not profitable to you, in any way.
It would be an uplift, for our nation.
If you, O King, agree, I'll write letters to all the provinces
On your authority." The king nodded, and handed Haman his ring—
The ring—as a stamp of approval—to set in motion—and to seal the thing.

Mordecai, on learning of the decree, rent his clothes,
Putting on sack-cloth and ashes—for all to see.
Word came to the queen that the old Jew who normally sat at the king's gate,
Was weeping and wailing, and bemoaning the Jewish fate.

On learning the whole story, even to the amount of cash involved,
The queen was alarmed but regretted that at present,
There was nothing she could do. For it was thirty days, since her last audience
With the king, and to enter the royal chambers unrequested,
Then death it was sure to bring, unless of course,
The king held out his golden sceptre
But it was a dangerous risk—should he not accept her.
Mordecai exercised his guardian right, saying, "You as queen
Must put up a fight. Don't think your death in this royal household
Will be prevented, when the extermination orders are implemented.
Who knoweth, that you have come to this kingdom, for such a time as this?

For if you do not have your say, then God will find some other way."

Now Esther's reply was, "I'll die if I must, but I and my maids
Will fast three days; we'll eat no food or drink no drink, that's what I say,
Now go you into Shushan, and order every Jewish woman, and man
To do the same; let them follow this very plan."

After three days Queen Esther, donned her royal robes,
And into the royal chambers, she timidly strode.
Would the king accept, or would he reject her?
Her face lit up, as he held out his golden sceptre.
She touched the tip, as such was the custom, then said,
"If it please the king, a banquet, I have prepared,
And I'd deem it a great honour, if you would attend, and be my guest.
Then I have a further request, if Prince Haman, could also be there,
And help us to dine on this sumptuous fare?"

Haman hurried home, in his dignified way, his face all beaming.
He'd got the king's approval—what else was there to say?
He'd also received an invitation to dine with the king and queen—
Just them and him alone—and not another guest to be seen.
Then his face changed, for there in his way, sat Mordecai,
Looking him full and square in the eyes, as if to say;
"I know your plans, and your wicked schemes, that you're about to play!"

So on entering his home, one look was enough, to tell Zeresh, his wife,
About the rebuff, "Oh, no, the king was fine, he agreed to my plan,
But on the way home, I met that man.
He sat there like my conscience, reminding me, what is good and just,
And what is just me. He infuriates me, and that's not all,
I long to be rid of him, and to see him fall."

"Well! Why not?" said Zeresh. "You're in a position to rid yourself of this irritation
It is your decision. Our grounds are big and wide, the fence is high.
There's plenty of room to build a scaffold to hang him, till he die."
"Good thinking, wife, you're way ahead, I'll start the workmen right away."
With a jubilant gait, he left the room, singing to himself a little tune.
"I'll build it there beneath the sky; fifty cubits shouldn't be too high."

The banquet proceeded as planned, and when the eating was over and done,
And when the conversations had really got started, the king said.
"Tell me, my queen, what is the petition you want of me? For it
Shall be granted, up to half of my kingdom."
Esther smiled a thank you, then said, "Thank you so much, my king,
I would that you do me the honour, of your presence—at another banquet—
Tomorrow, and Prince Haman I'd like you to bring."

That night the king could not sleep, perhaps his conscience,
Or what he did eat, whatever it was, he uneasily lay.
He longed for the time, when it would be day. He called his chamberlain to read
To him, from the Medo-Persian chronicles to pass the time away.
They came upon the entry of the prevented assassination of the king.
By one Mordecai. "Stop," said the king.
"What honour was placed upon this man, for his zeal and diligence?"
"None," said the chamberlain, "for there is none recorded by the occurrence."

The king arose, asking what officials were in court, this day.
"There is Haman—Your Majesty, he has just arrived."
"Good," said the king. "Send him in, we'll see him right away."
Now Haman had arrived early, to petition the king to hang Mordecai.
On the new gallows he'd erected—seventy-five feet high.

"Ah!" said the king. "Haman, you are just the man. Tell me,
How should the king honour a man, in whom the king delighteth?
Tell me, if you can." (Now Haman mentally preened himself, and stood his full height.
The king must mean me, for I am in favour, for I try, with all my might.)

"Let him wear royal robes that the king has worn;
And let him ride upon the king's horse with a crown upon his head.
And let one of the royal princes lead the horse; and while it is led,
Proclaim the words, 'Thus shall the king honour the man in whom the king delighteth.' "

The king nodded. "Thank you, Haman, well said. Now go and
get the robes, and the
Crown, and the horse, and take them to Mordecai.
For I am well pleased with him, thus say I."

Haman led the king's horse, as the king had commanded him to
do,
With Mordecai sitting astride it, and looking really regal,
For he was wearing the king's robe, and a royal crown upon his
head:
And what was more; Haman was reciting, the things that had to
be said.

When Haman arrived home sometime later, he was very dismal
and forlorn,
His chin hung low; it was easy to know, that his pride had taken
a fall.
His advisers, on learning his news, told him that he could not
win,
By trying to outsmart the Jews, for they as a nation, must prosper,
Whatever their situation.
While Haman was licking his wounds (or soothing his sorrows,
it's more correct to say),
A messenger came from the palace saying, that the banquet was
under way!

After the meal, the king said, "And now, queen, what is it you
really wanted to say?"
"I plead for my life, Your Majesty; and I plead for those of my
race,
For that man there, has issued a decree, to exterminate us all, all
in a single day."

The king reversed the order, by issuing a further decree,
And the ring that had been given to Haman, was retrieved,
And issued to Mordecai; in order to seal that decree.
The outcome of all that followed, was plain for all to see.
God is with His people, wherever they may be.
For the Jews were a captive race, and in captivity.
Through God they triumphed, in their cause, and that,
    victoriously.
For they turned on the anti-Jews—and had the victory.

Five hundred they slew in Shushan, and seventy-five thousand
    throughout the provinces.
Haman was hanged on his own gallows—along with the ten sons
    of his.
His house and his property, were given to Mordecai.
For God had chosen the man, to avert His people.
From an untimely end, and contrary to His plan.

(It is also well to note that many of the inhabitants,
Because of their fear, they, themselves became Jews.
For they had discovered, that there was none who could stand
    against them.)

Shadrach, Meshach, and Abed-nego

In Judah, in the days when Jehoiakim was king,
Babylonian armies besieged the land, and captured everything.
But Nebuchadnezzar was selective, selective in what he took,
And amongst his selection of prizes, four young men he took.

Their names were Daniel, Hananiah, Mishael, and Azariah,
But names can be changed, as soon they were; but not so their faith in God.
For they had learned from a very young age—of God's provision and guidance,
And which was the path to be trod.

Once they arrived in Babylon, they were selected once again.
For Nebuchadnezzar had issued an order, and had made it very plain.
A school was set up—and for the prospective candidate
The enrollment had to be precise. No others would relate.
No blemish permitted, students must be well-favoured.
Skillful in all wisdom, cunning in knowledge and understanding
Aptitude for science, and an ability to stand before the king,
And those he would dwell among.
Also, be able to learn and teach others, of the Chaldean tongue.

Provision would be made of victuals—and a daily portion would be put aside;
From the king's very own meat and wine.
So, no lack of nourishment, would hinder their learning—they should do, just fine.
There was to be adequate accommodation—and the course included three years of probabtion.

Now of the captives selected, were Daniel and his mates.
And Ashpenaz (the master of the eunuchs) interviewed all the candidates.
And he set Melzar over them—and also changed their names.
Daniel became Belteshazzar—a Chaldean name as all could see.
Hananiah, Mishael, and Azariah became Shadrach, Meshach, and Abed-nego,
And that, respectively.

Daniel, on learning the king's rule, of the sumptuous meat, and wine,
Asked for an interview with Melzar, and just upon that score,
Saying, "Although I'm speaking myself, I speak for all us four
We are Hebrews, and serve the God of heaven, and although we truly
Honour the king, we cannot obey him in this thing.
We ask you a favour in this matter; don't serve us with the king's meat and wine.
Water and pulse, will do just fine—you can rely on us
For silence, we promise not to chatter."

Melzar answered, that he could lose his head; for doing just, what Daniel said.
"You ask too much; it can't be done; I'm placed in charge
Of your welfare, and have only just begun."
Daniel said, "Prove thy servants, with a test; make a ten-day trial on pulse and
Water; then compare us with the other candidates.
Then see for yourself, who comes out best."
Melzar pondered, as he stroked his chin, then slowly acquiesed.
The trial proved positive for Daniel and his mates;
For their countenances were fairer, and fatter, than the other candidates.
So Melzar was pleased with the decision, as well should he be.

He nodded his head, in approval, saying, "The arrangement will stand.
For you look all fine to me."

As with their nourishment their studies too, were rewarded.
For God honours those who trust Him, and feign would do His will.
For God gave His four children, much learning in all wisdom, knowledge, and skill.
Nebuchadnezzar found that the four communed best and were ten times better
Than his magicians and astrologers, in any kind of test.

But Nebuchadnezzar was so full of pride, on all that had come to him.
He thought all credit was due to him, alone, and that boasting was no sin.
He ordered a huge statue to be made—and that to be of gold.
Sixty cubits high, by six cubits wide, and on the plain of Dura to be erected.
The dedication to be attended by all—princes, governors, captains,
Judges, treasurers, counsellors, sheriffs, and rulers—excuses were noneffective.

A further command was issued—and that, to be obeyed by all.
That at any time, on hearing the sound of music, all must stop, and on their faces
Fall, making obeisance and worshiping the statue that the king, Nebuchadnezzar,
Had set up, on the Durian plain. Music included the cornet, flute,
Harp, sackbut, psaltery, and dulcimer, and even if just worshiped—
Bow down, and do it all again.

Punishment for non-compliance, was to be most severe;
Culprits would be burned alive, it was announced for all to hear.
Punishment would be swift and sure, no one would be excused.
Let the offenders tremble; excuses would be counted as abuse.
In this matter, all had to obey the king, as in everything.

It wasn't long before the Chaldean spies, set out to trap the Jews,
For jealousy is a wicked sin, and when combined with self-ambition,
It isn't long before you score a win, if you know the Jewish tradition.
Three culprits were brought before the king—their accusers had broad grins.
"We caught them all standing up erect, Your Majesty—just when the music begins."

Nebuchadnezzar listened, and thinking to himself, how could the accusers be
Certain, and truthful, on what they said they'd found.
For they themselves, if complying, would have their faces to the ground.
So turning to the accused, he said, "Is it true Shadrach, Meshach, and Abed-nego
That you failed to obey a lawful command, by not worshiping the golden image,
That I set up within my land?"

They answered out boldly, for fear is not of God.
"We did not bow down to your idol, for we worship the living God."
Nebuchadnezzar, to show his mercy, said he'd give them another chance,

Providing that in future, they would adhere to the statute law—if
   not perchance,
"You'll just take the consequence." Then Nebuchadnezzar added,
"And who is that God, that shall deliver you, out of my hands?"

Shadrach, Meshach, and Abed-nego answered the king, "O
   Nebuchadnezzar,
What we say, is not idle chatter, we are not careful to answer you
   in this matter.
If it be so, our God whom we serve is able to deliver us, from
The burning fiery furnace, and He will deliver us, out of thy
   hand, O King.
But if not, be it known unto thee, O King,
That we will not serve thy gods, nor worship the golden image,
   which thou hast set up."

Nebuchadnezzar reddened; his face was full of fury; he was the
   king;
How dare they speak thus, his words would end the story!
He gave the command that the furnace be made one seven times
   hotter,
Than first planned.
The most mighty men, that the army could hire
Had to bind them tightly, before throwing them into the fire.

The furnace was hot, exceedingly hot, that it slew
The would-be slayers; this was a drama, a living spectacle,
And the faithful Jews, the players.
People stood aghast, as they watched the views.
And with heart-felt thanks that they were not in their shoes.

Nebuchadnezzar gazed with mouth agape, and peered for a
   closer view,
Saying to his counsellors around him, "Tell me, if it's not true,

Did we not throw three men bound, into that fearsome blaze?
For I see four men loose, and walking in the haze, and they have
 no hurt!
And the fourth is like the Son of God."

The king trembled as he watched, shouting low, but his voice
 rose higher.
"Come forth, Shadrach, Meshach, and Abed-nego." And without
 a second bidding
Out they walked, from the midst of the fire.

The miracle that had been witnessed, was still evident for all to
 see,
For there was no trace of fire upon them, not a singed hair, to tell.
Even their clothing was free, for none of it carried the smell!

Nebuchadnezzar's face had changed as he said to the company,
"Blessed be the God of Shadrach, Meshach, and
 Abed-nego—who sent His angel,
And delivered His servants; I make a new decree.

"Any that speak amiss against the God of Shadrach, Mesach, and
 Abed-nego,
Shall be cut in pieces and their homes demolished,
For no other god can deliver like this."

The Writing on the Wall

Belshazzar, he loved feasting, amongst other things as well.
"Why not?" he'd say, "I am the king," and then his chest would swell.
His father had been mighty, and conquered many lands.
Taken many captives, and led them forth in bands.

He'd even sacked Jerusalem, and robbed its Holy Temple;
Bringing back the gold and silver cups, to store as an example.
Nebuchadnezzar had not used the cups, but kept them safe, away.
He thought of them as trophies, of when he'd won the day

But Belshazzar, his son, had pride, and arrogance as well,
He cared for no one, he was the king, then his chest would swell.
One night Belshazzar decided to proclaim a feast. "Invite all the princes, their ladies,
And their concubines—that's the thing!
Bring on the dancing girls, with music, let the feast go with a swing."

The wine it flowed freely, as did the boasting too;
Each trying to outboast the other, just telling what they knew, one shouting,
Whilst another trying to proclaim, attempting to shout down the other,
Which would bring him instant fame.

The king nodded his approval, as he listened, and drank his wine as well.
Then he thought quite deeply, and his chest began to swell.
"Bring in the cups of gold, and silver, my father won long ago,
The wine it should taste sweeter, and even add to its glow."

But the cups he'd asked for were sacred, and placed aside by God,
Awaiting their reinstatement, when Judah homeward trod.
Belshazzar noted their distribution, to himself as well as his guests.
He raised his cup to his lips, and drank quite gustily.
"You know," he said, "this wine tastes better, I feel quite merrily—"
Then he staggered to his feet, and raised his cup once more.

He smiled at his courtiers, one and all, then glanced towards the door—
Then his face changed colour, as his gaze lingered on the wall.
His legs they would not hold him, then he sagged upon the floor. Staggering
To his feet, he looked at the wall again, what he thought he saw,
But wasn't sure, was there, and very plain. A hand writing, words.

And what was more, their meaning was unknown to all.
Belshazzar's knees began to knock; he clutched the table lest he should fall.
His pride was hurt, he was in shock, his fear-bound eyes watched the hand,
As it wrote upon the wall. His pride was gone, that was true, for it goeth before a fall.

The king stammered, "Who—can interpret its meaning. Tell me, tell me, tell
Me now—I'll give a robe, a golden chain, and elevate to third in the land.
I'll keep my word, that I vow."

But none in court knew the score, so none in the court could say;
So Belshazzar trembled all the more, for he knew in his heart,
  that he'd had his day.

Jonah

Now Jonah was a prophet, and gave out the Word of God,
But Jonah was also human, and the human road he trod.
For he himself, had a will of his own—and like all wilful humans,
He reaped, what he had sown.

Disobedience was his shortcoming, for God had given him a word;
To go to Nineveh, that great city, and tell them, what he'd heard.
God was judging Nineveh, for their sin was great,
But Jonah knew that God was merciful so he'd leave them to their fate.

Jonah decided to run, to get away from God's plan;
But he was a chosen vessel, and this was the will of God,
And not the will of man.

He went down to the water side, to watch the pounding of the wave.
He'd get away from it all, for Nineveh was a city that someone else could save.
Why should he get involved? It wasn't his own town,
Why should he do it? Then a smile lit up his frown.

There was a ship all ready to sail, its cargo already on board.
It was going to Tarshish— a long way—quite a place to hide.
He paid his fare to the crew, he might even enjoy the ride.
He found a place below deck, where he could stow his gear.
He wasn't feeling seasick, but he felt a little queer.
So he lay down in a corner, and soon was fast asleep.

The crew were about their duties, when a storm rose on the deep.
They battened down the hatches, securing all they could,
But the storm was not abating, and they didn't feel too good.
"Let each man call on his own god," the captain shouted with all his might,
"For I fear that someone aboard my ship, is responsible for our plight."

Each of the crew called on his god, which didn't quell the sea.
"Let's cast lots," said one man, "And find out whom it may be."
Lots were cast, and Jonah was selected, as the cause of all the trouble.
The captain went below to accuse him, and found him in a huddle.
Jonah was curled up fast asleep, and the captain quite annoyed.

"Wake up, you sluggard, and call on your God, see if He can help,
To calm the sea—we've already lightened the ship—
And I'm far too young yet for eternity. What's your trade anyway?
And whom are you running from? For you are on the run,
I can tell at a glance—and you didn't come aboard by chance!"

Jonah confessed, that he'd run away, from doing as God had instructed,
For he'd been told to go to Ninevah and was running the other way.
His calling was that of a prophet, God's mouthpiece, so to say.
He was the cause of all the trouble, causing their terrible plight.
"It wouldn't have happened if I'd done my job, and not resorted to flight.
The only thing you can do, Captain," said Jonah dismally,
"Is to take me and my belongings, and throw us in the sea."

The crew thought the punishment hard and tried with all their might,
To row their ship near to land, but they soon gave up the fight.
The winds were contrary, and the gale force did increase—
So over the side they pushed Jonah, to see if it would bring them peace.

But God is merciful, as Jonah knew. God had already conceived a plan,
To create a large fish to swallow Jonah, and thus to save the man.

What were Jonah's feelings, as he slipped quickly through the fish's gullet?
Was he a morsel sought after, as herring, cod, and mullet?
It must have been quite dark inside, and enough to make one feel queer;
But what a relief, to find he could still breathe, in that warm, clammy atmosphere.

His thoughts must have been many, for he still had time to think.
He had run away from the will of God—and how low, can a man sink?
If only he had his time over he'd take a different course.
He'd find his way to Nineveh—he'd even go by horse.

Then he started praying—praying with all his heart.
He told God of his predicament (who knew it, from the start).
But one thing that is marvellous—most marvellous to me.
That God hears our prayers, when we pray, wherever we may be:
Whether we are on the mountain top—or right in the depths of the sea.

After three days and nights, Jonah was feeling worse for wear.
At least, he could still breathe, that smelly, tainted air.
Then God in His mercy, He saw fit to cause the fish
To swim to land, and cause that fish to vomit,
Depositing Jonah there, right on the golden sand.

It must have been wonderful to breathe that sweet fresh air
And breathe it deep within.
Jonah in his heart was sorry he'd been so wrong to sin.
Off to Nineveh he hastened, he went there without delay.
Now Nineveh was a big place, sixty miles in circumference.
At last Jonah reached the city, and journeyed in it for a day.
Then he gave his message—and very strong words they were;
Because they were so wicked, in forty days' time—would be the
    end of Nineveh!

People were startled by the word, prophesied to them.
The king of Nineveh heard it too, and was alarmed as other men.
Then the king repented, ordering everyone to do the same:
Everyone must fast from food and water, from the lowest to
    those of fame.
The fast applied to man and beast—everyone the same.

Meanwhile, Jonah built a booth for himself. It was outside the
    city,
For the sun was hot, beating down on him, encouraging his
    self-pity.
To aid his comfort God allowed a gourd to grow, affording him
    complete shelter,
Which was very fine for him, but teaching was to follow.
God provided a cut-worm, which destroyed the gourd and most
    of the shelter
That it did afford—and making Jonah squirm.

The forty days came and went—and the city was not destroyed
While Jonah suffered as the sun beat down, he was most annoyed.
"I knew God was merciful," Jonah said, "and as soon as they started to repent,
God forgave them, as He always does—
Why, I've wasted that time that I've spent!"
But that time was only wasted, in Jonah's mind, for God had accomplished His plan.
The people had repented, and been forgiven.
And fellowship established between God and man.

Choice

I did not ask to be born, I simply had no choice.
And what to me was coercion, caused my parents to rejoice.
But I had arrived, and that for sure; it was up to me to do my best,
And then, perhaps a little more.

Then the flags were flying, as the country was at war,
And I was in that age group, sent out to settle the score.
I had to go—I had no choice, no argument, or could not even
    raise my voice,
I simply had to go, no choice.

When on the battlefield, mid screams, and bursting shell,
With conflagration all around, a scene of a miniature Hell.
Men and boys were dying, their destinations all unknown.
Had I known then then, what I know now, there is *one* who can
    atone.

We can have salvation, and know where we are bound.
Jesus is the answer, for grace in Him is found.
He is the way—the truth—the life—His word is very plain.
He is the only way to the Father, and a place in heaven gain.

Though we have no choice for our natural birth, we can be born
    again.
So stop, think hard, and ponder, and take a little pause.
There is a way to heaven—and the choice is yours.

Don't Miss the Bus

My mother pulled me by the hand, and said that we must rush.
I looked at her in surprise, thinking, *Why the fuss?*
We hurried on, then I fell; oh! we'll miss the bus!

We were living in the Wop-wop's, and now I know why all the
    fuss,
Our means of transport, had gone on its way—in fact we'd
    missed the bus.
The next scheduled, was for the next day, our plight a true reality.
And I had learned a lesson, that of punctuality.

As I grew up, a war came, and I was in the army.
I learned discipline, and as I told my girl,
She said she thought me barmy.
The time came for me to catch my train, but my girl clung to my
collar. "Don't go, my love, don't go! Or you'll make me holler!"
I missed my train! But when I got back,
The sergeant he was livid; he spoke to me, in no uncertain terms.
His language—it was vivid. "You're not fit to leave the camp,
Or to be at large; look at your uniform, you're a disgrace,
And you're on a charge!"

Then I was posted overseas, where the fighting was at its height.
The going was rough, and very tough, but I fought with all my
    might.
One day a reprieve came, and I was selected to travel home.
Oh! The joy of the prospects of a trip upon the foam.
I decided to celebrate with a night out upon the town.

Oh—my head, it suffered, and my dignity as well,
For here I was left in a land remote—as gossiping tongues would tell.
Once again I was deprived of hope, as once more I'd missed the boat.

Oh, the lessons that we must learn, and the discipline we should not spurn—
But lessons still had to be taught to me
For when the next ship left, with me upon the sea,
Up came some ships from the Jap navy.

Our ship was slow, so we could not run,
The grinning Japs, they had their fun, I was hit on the head.
They put out my lamp, I ended the war in a prison camp.

But internment is not without some consolation, one learns to think,
But without elation, I'd missed the bus, I'd missed the train,
I'd missed the boat, but never again.

Life is short, but it's not the end. I learned of this, from a friend.
There is a road that we can take, which will lead to life,
And that's for sure, and we can live forever more.

So listen, my friend, to the words I say, for Jesus said,
"I am the truth, the life, and the way."
So, my friend, don't procrastinate.
For when you're dead, it is too late.

Join the Queue

"What are you waiting for, in this queue?"
"I'm waiting behind her, for she looks as if she knew!"
She smiled, and she nodded. "Yes, that is true,
And I'm behind him, who's been here for a while,
And he knows what he's doing; just look at his smile."

Then I approached smiler to see if he knew.
"Well, there were people before me, who stood in this queue,
And no one would tell me, why they stood in this line,
So I joined on the end, and I'm doing fine,
I'll know when I get there, I'll find out, by and by,
I'm in no hurry, I've got till I die."

Yes, people do, just form a long line,
It's custom to do it, when they have the time,
So follow the line that knows where it's going,
Look at their faces, and if they are glowing,
Listen to their talk, and if it's of God,
You'll learn of the line, where our Saviour has trod.

Go hand in hand with your friends, and husband or wife,
Follow Jesus' line, for His Word says that
"I am the way, the truth, and the life."

The Piper

When I was young, in days gone by, I listened to many a tale,
Some were good, and some were bad, and some would make
 you wail.

Now one of the tales, that was told to me, was a Piper, dressed so
 colourfully.
Where he originated, no one knew; nor did anyone ask.
He just appeared, and that was that.
He boasted much, saying "I can solve any task."

He said he'd cleared a town of rats, when everything else had
 failed.
But when the authorities had refused to pay, he whistled his pipe,
 saying, "You'll rue the day."

He changed his tune upon his pipe; the children began to dance,
 and run.
They followed him wherever he went; all was joyous, all was
 fun.

But the children were never seen again, not to this very day.
It is a story, so I'm told, so of it's truth, I cannot say.

But one thing that I do know, which is true, that the Piper
 appears in many ways,
And constantly changes his tune, just to suit the occasion,
No matter how many he slays.

He appears in our towns and cities, and in our countryside,
On our hills and beaches, comes in on the rising tide.

His tunes attract the young folk, they sway, as they take on the beat,
They fling their arms, saying, "Yeah, yeah, yeah," they think it's cool or neat.

The older folk just sigh or take on a deafened pose,
"It's sad to see," say the thoughtful ones; while others watch, then turn up their nose.

"They're only young once," others say, "let them have their fun,
Life's too short to be serious, and for them it's just begun."

But little they know of the Piper's leading, or where the dance will end.
They're brainwashed into thinking, that the Piper is a friend.

The Piper's dress is colourful, it comes in many hues,
He takes on many guises, drugs, music, and booze.

People, do not be dazzled by him, or ensnared by his train,
For he's on a runaway mission, and your end will be the same.

He's a wolf in sheep's clothing, a curse and not a boon, remember,
If you employ the Piper, you must also pay for the tune.

Turn from his murderous deceits, for there is another way,
Learn to live for tomorrow, and not only for today.